PET SOS

**ARGYLL & BUTE COUNCIL
LIBRARY AND INFORMATION SERVICES**

Books should be returned on or before the date above
Renewals may be made by personal application,
post or telephone, if not in demand

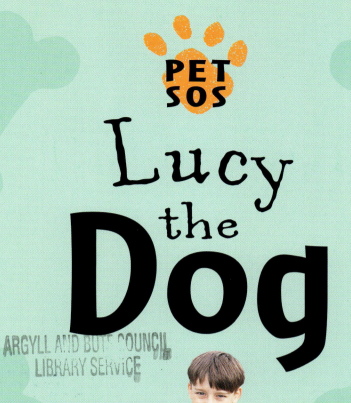

PET SOS

Lucy the Dog

Tamsin Osler

Photography by Chris Fairclough

W

FRANKLIN WATTS
LONDON • SYDNEY

This edition 2004

First published in Great Britain by
Franklin Watts
96 Leonard Street
London EC2A 4XD

Franklin Watts Australia
45–51 Huntley Street
Alexandria NSW 2015

© 2001 Franklin Watts

ISBN: 0 7496 5600 X
Dewey Decimal Classification 636.7
A CIP catalogue record for this book is available from the British Library

Printed in Malaysia

Planning and production by Discovery Books
Editors: Tamsin Osler, Kate Banham
Design: Ian Winton
Art Direction: Jason Anscomb
Photography: Chris Fairclough

Acknowledgements
The publishers would like to thank Mr and Mrs Bagley, their children George
and Alice, the staff at NCDL Roden Rehoming Centre and the NCDL for their
help in the production of this book.

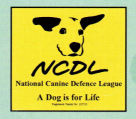

NCDL
National Canine Defence League
A Dog is for Life
Registered Charity No. 227523

CONTENTS

Meet Lucy

This is Lucy, a **border collie**. She lives at a National **Canine** Defence League (NCDL) **rehoming** centre at Roden. She was brought here by the police when she was picked up as a **stray**.

Border collies were originally used to herd, or round up, cattle and sheep. This is why they are also known as working dogs.

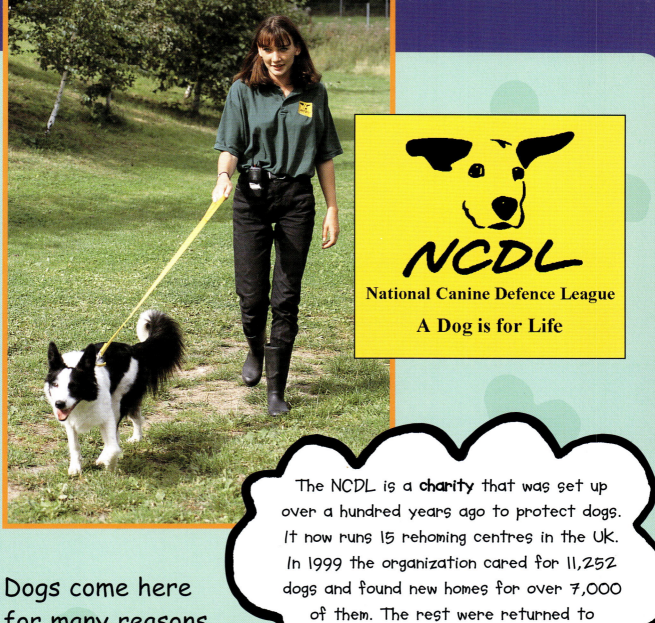

NCDL

National Canine Defence League

A Dog is for Life

The NCDL is a **charity** that was set up over a hundred years ago to protect dogs. It now runs 15 rehoming centres in the UK. In 1999 the organization cared for 11,252 dogs and found new homes for over 7,000 of them. The rest were returned to their owners or stayed with the NCDL.

Dogs come here for many reasons. Some are here because their owners don't want them or because they can't look after them any more. A lot of dogs come because they were found abandoned.

Roden Rehoming Centre

There may be as many as 140 dogs and puppies at Roden. They are housed in different blocks. There is a 'nursery' for the puppies, a 'recovery' area for sick dogs, and a 'new arrivals' block. There is also a block for the dogs who are ready to go to new homes.

This puppy arrived at Roden with an injured leg.

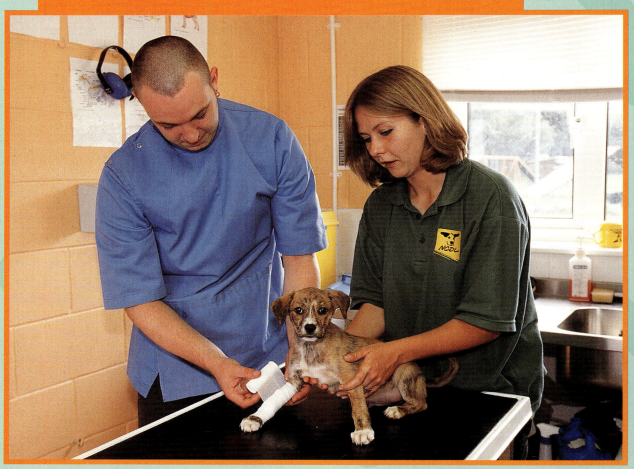

All the dogs are vaccinated against a number of dog diseases. They are also tagged. A small electronic **microchip**, or tag, with a **unique** number is placed under the skin on the back of the dog's neck.

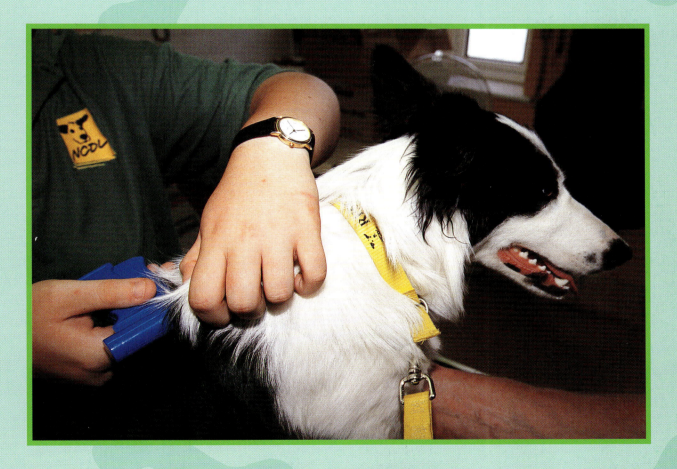

When a **scanner** is passed over the microchip, it reads this number. If Lucy got lost, this number would help the police to find out where she lives.

Each member of staff looks after a different block at the centre. They have to feed, **groom**, bath and exercise the dogs, as well as give them any medicine they may need.

Most dogs like having their coats groomed.

New arrivals at the centre are usually given a bath.

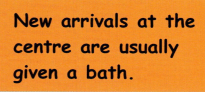

The dogs at Roden are walked at least once a day. Some, like Lucy, are walked on a lead. Others are allowed to run around off the lead in an enclosed **compound**.

Before a dog is rehomed, the NCDL take it to a busy place, such as a car park, to make sure that the dog is well–behaved and not scared by all the people and cars.

Roden has 25 acres of grounds. There are fields and woods, and even a small pond with ducks.

A visit to Roden

This is George Bagley and his younger sister Alice. George and his family used to have a dog but it became ill and died some months ago. Now they want to get a new dog. Mr Bagley, a farmer, is keen to have a **rescue dog**.

The NCDL has sent George lots of information about adopting and caring for rescue dogs.

The Bagleys have heard about NCDL's Roden Rehoming Centre and decide to visit it. A member of staff shows them the dogs that are ready for rehoming.

Alice would like to take home every puppy she sees at the rehoming centre!

George and his family are introduced to Lucy. Being a border collie, Lucy needs lots of exercise. She needs a home with plenty of space. A farm is a good place for her.

The NCDL always tries to find the right home for the dogs in its care. A big dog might not be suitable in a small house. A nervous dog would not be suitable in a home where there are young children.

The family are taken to a 'Meet and Greet' room, where they can spend time getting to know Lucy in a place that looks like home. The room has a sofa and chairs, a dog bed and an old television. There is even a refrigerator and a sink with running water.

A few days later, an NCDL rehoming officer visits the Bagleys' farm. He needs to make sure that Lucy will be happy there. He approves of the farm, and asks the Bagleys to collect Lucy as soon as they can.

Next day, all the family set off to fetch Lucy. Everyone is excited.

If your family is about to get a new dog, decide beforehand where your dog will sleep, and where you will put its food and water bowls. You should also decide which parts of the house and garden your dog will be allowed in.

George and his family have already bought most of the things their new dog will need. She has a feeding bowl, a brush, a plastic bed and some dog food. George has chosen some toys for her, and a bright red lead.

Lucy loves playing with George and Alice. One of her favourite games is playing tug-of-war with George.

Although Lucy is still only a puppy, she is very strong. She mustn't be allowed to 'win' too often. She will respect George more if he remains in control of her.

George throws a frisbee and a ball for Lucy to fetch. These are better than a stick because they are soft and won't harm Lucy's teeth or jam in her throat.

Playing with Lucy encourages her to think quickly.

George and Lucy play for a long time, but Lucy never seems to get tired. George tires long before she does.

Training Lucy

George is teaching Lucy to obey simple commands. He teaches her to understand the words 'sit', 'stay' and 'heel'.

George rewards Lucy with special dog treats each time she does what he says. Rewarding her is an important part of the training process.

Mr Bagley wants Lucy to get used to being near the other animals on the farm. He puts on Lucy's lead, and quietly and carefully takes her into a field with cows. Lucy is both **cautious** and excited by them.

The cows are more curious than nervous when they see Lucy.

Before George takes Lucy for a walk, he always puts the lead on her.

By law, every dog in Britain must wear an **identification** disc attached to its collar. This shows the dog owner's name and address.

Lucy is taken out for a walk every day. Dogs that don't get enough exercise may become difficult to handle and start being naughty.

Lucy is happy and healthy in her new home. She is enjoying her new life on the Bagleys' farm, and has become a much loved member of the family.

The NCDL encourages new owners of their rehomed dogs to send in a photograph of the dog in its new home. They sometimes telephone the new owners to check that the dog is well. They may also invite the owners to dog shows and open days at their centres.

Glossary

Border collie	A type of dog. Other well-known breeds include poodles and spaniels.
Canine	The word used to describe everything to do with dogs.
Cautious	Taking care, being careful.
Charity	An organization, such as the NCDL, that raises money for a particular cause.
Circulation	The continous movement of blood around the body.
Compound	An enclosed area.
Groom	To brush or comb an animal's coat.
Identification	Something that tells people who you are and where you live.
Microchip	A tiny electronic device.
Parasites	Tiny animals that live on and feed off other animals.
Rehome	To find a new home for a person or animal.
Rescue dog	A dog that has been rescued by an animal welfare charity.
Routine	A regular way of doing things.
Scanner	An electronic device that can 'read' information stored on a microchip.
Stray	An animal that has been abandoned or has got lost.
Unique	Something is said to be unique when it is the only one of its kind.
Vaccinate	To give medicine or treatment that protects against diseases.
Worms	Small parasites that live in the stomachs of other animals. When an animal is wormed it is given medicine to get rid of the worms in its stomach.

Further information

The NCDL runs 15 rehoming centres which you can visit free of charge. To find out which days they are open for visiting, contact your closest branch on one of the numbers below:

Ballymena
Co Antrim
028 2565 2977

Bridgend
Mid-Glamorgan
01656 725219

Canterbury
Kent
01227 792505

Darlington
Co Durham
01325 333114

Evesham
Worcestershire
01386 830613

Ilfracombe
North Devon
01271 812709

Kenilworth
Warwickshire
01926 484398

Leeds
Yorkshire
0113 2613194

Liverpool
Merseyside
0151 480 0660

Newbury
Berkshire
01488 658391

Roden
Telford, Shropshire
01952 770225

Salisbury
Wiltshire
01980 629634

Shoreham
West Sussex
01273 452576

Snetterton
Norfolk
01953 498377

West Calder
Edinburgh
01506 873459

Or you can contact their head office at:

NCDL
17 Wakley Street
London EC1V 7RQ
020 7837 0006
Web site: www.ncdl.org.uk

Australian organizations

Oz Dog rescue
www.ozdogrescue.com

Save-A-Dog-Scheme Inc
PO Box 78
East Caulfield, VIC 3145
Tel: (03) 9885 1188

Australian Animal
Protection Society
10 Homeleigh Road
Keysborough, VIC 3173
Email: enquiries@aaps.org.au

RSPCA Australia
PO Box 265
Deakin West ACT 2600
Tel: (02) 6282 8300
www.rspca.org.au

Index